A LETTER TO MY FAMILY

A Journey through Persecution in Nazi Germany, Refuge in Shanghai, and New Life in America

as told by
LISA JOHNSON

A Letter to My Family
Copyright © 2024—Lisa Johnson

Published by Free Agent Press

All rights reserved. This book is protected by the copyright laws of the United States of America. This book may not be copied or reprinted for commercial gain or profit. The use of short quotations or occasional page copying for personal or group study is permitted and encouraged. Permission will be granted upon request.

Maps created with MapChart.net under a Creative Commons Attribution-ShareAlike 4.0 International License.

Edited by: Heather Woosley

ISBN: 978-1-946730-28-2 (hardback)
ISBN: 978-1-946730-29-9 (paperback)
ISBN: 978-1-946730-30-5 (ebook)

 Published by Free Agent Press
FreeAgentPress.com
Satsuma, Alabama 36572
VID: 20240421

For Walter
May his memory be a blessing

CONTENTS

Preface 1
About Me 5
War and More 15
Music and Marriage 19
Taken Away 24
Time to Go 26
Never Enough 30
Where in the World Is Shanghai? 33
Providential 36
Living in the Jewish District 39
News from Home 43
Home Fires Are Burning 45
Even Worse 48
To the U.S.A. 52
Toward the Future 62
Photo Gallery 66
The Family Today in Their Own Words 72
Gittel's Epilogue: July 2023 77
The Journey from Walter's Perspective 82
Epilogue 91

Preface

A Letter to My Family

WHAT DOES IT MEAN to save your own life? These words usually relate to survival itself, but may occasionally refer to a reinventing of one's own life. For Walter Berger, saving his life meant both of these things, but there was a literal aspect as well. Walter saved everything that came his way materially, and in doing so, gave us a tangible representation of a remarkable lifetime.

Walter Berger did not set out to be remarkable, but as he was caught up in world events, his instinctive and careful preservation documented his life—suggesting another way to "save" your own life. Images inspire narrative, and in the pages that follow, I bear witness to Walter Berger's Holocaust journey through a narrative inspired by some 50 images—all of which are housed in the Berger Burns Collection of St. Louis's Kaplan Feldman Holocaust Museum.

First, Walter's story is told, in what could have been Walter's own words, in the form of a letter to his living family. Here I play the part of ventriloquist, and hope that the words I offer as "Walter's" (suggested by the collection itself) will honor his experience. Later, the backstory of this project and how it came to be is revealed, along with a photo gallery of images from the collection at the St. Louis Holocaust Museum. The Berger Burns Collection illustrates in the first-person what bravery and resilience is all about.

Walter Berger saved his life indeed.

Lisa Johnson
October 9, 2023

Preface

To my beloved family:

I am your loving Zeyde—that's "Grandpa" in Yiddish. I would have loved to tell you this story in person, maybe sitting together in the back yard in Staunton by the pool while playing with the dogs. I wish I could tell you what it was like for your family, how it is you came to be born where you were, and how it is that you are here now. Our story is an immigration story. I suppose no two immigrant stories are ever alike, and ours is certainly not a typical German account. This is how it happened for us, and I'd like to tell you about it in my own words.

—Your Zeyde, Walter Berger
(as interpreted by Lisa Johnson)

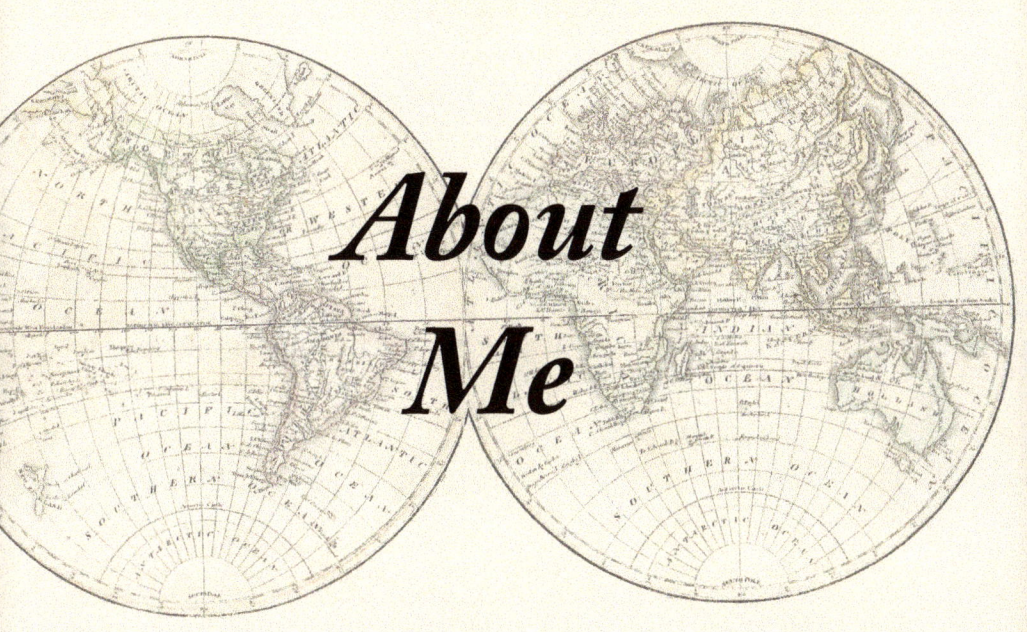

About Me

MY NAME IS OSKAR Walter Berger (I always liked to go by my middle name). Most of the papers and documents you will find about me call me Walter, though sometimes you will see "Oskar" first or second. You will often see "Israel" too, which is what the German government required us to add to our passports to identify ourselves as Jewish. Here is my reissued Nazi-era passport. Note the large "J" (for Jude) superimposed on the left page. When Hitler came to power in 1933, the Nazis wanted to distinguish those they considered to be of a "pureblooded German" race from those they considered to be of inferior races. Re-issuing passports to indicate racial identity was one of their ways of publicly differentiating groups of people. It was appalling to go through this process of being reissued a document declaring that I was a substandard resident of my own country as I had never held a sense of any difference among the races or a concept of hierarchy among people. But as it came to pass, the new devalued passport was only

one of the many humiliations that the Jewish people were forced to endure. Ultimately the Nazis disqualified Jews altogether as citizens of Germany. But before the terror came, I lived a normal, happy life.

I was born in Upper Silesia, Prussia (a region of northeast Germany) on January 12, 1896. The name of the town in those days was Beuthen, a bustling industrial district and mineral-rich site for coal and iron ore. Its population of 60,000 consisted of mostly Jewish inhabitants and merchants, but there were many Czechs living in Beuthen, as both Czechoslovakia and Poland were nearby. In the Second World War, some national boundaries were

redrawn when the Germans seized new territories to expand their Empire, pushing the boundary of a prospective German Reich ever further east. Today, this part of Silesia, including Beuthen, is not in Germany at all—it is now considered part of Poland and is called Bytom, with a population of 160,000.

About Me

My parents were Rosalie (née Freund, born in 1859) and Abraham Berger (born in 1860). I was the fifth of six children—three girls and three boys—and we were raised in the Jewish faith, as was typical for that area. Our parents didn't give us Hebrew names, though they had them themselves (Rachel and Abvraham).

Rosalie Berger

Abraham Berger

My father was devout and attended synagogue regularly. I remember him reading religious texts and prayers in Hebrew and observing the Jewish holidays. My inward-looking father did not talk much about what was personally meaningful to him, religious or otherwise, so I must rely on my memory of witnessing his religious habits. I have no record of either of my parents' personal reflections. They were typical conservative Germans of their day who worked hard and sent the children to school at the Beuthen Synagogue.

Our father's family started a general store called Gebrüder Berger (Berger Brothers) and built it up from a modest shop to a thriving business serving the entire city of Beuthen.

Walter is second from the right in this photo.

I was always quiet and careful about things. You might even say I was serious-minded. I was so scrupulous that I kept my Beuthen Synagogue religious school report cards reflecting my good grades.

They made me feel proud that I was following in my father's footsteps—maybe that's when I got in the habit of keeping all my important papers. Little did I know back then that holding on to letters and documents would mean so much later when telling the story of my life.

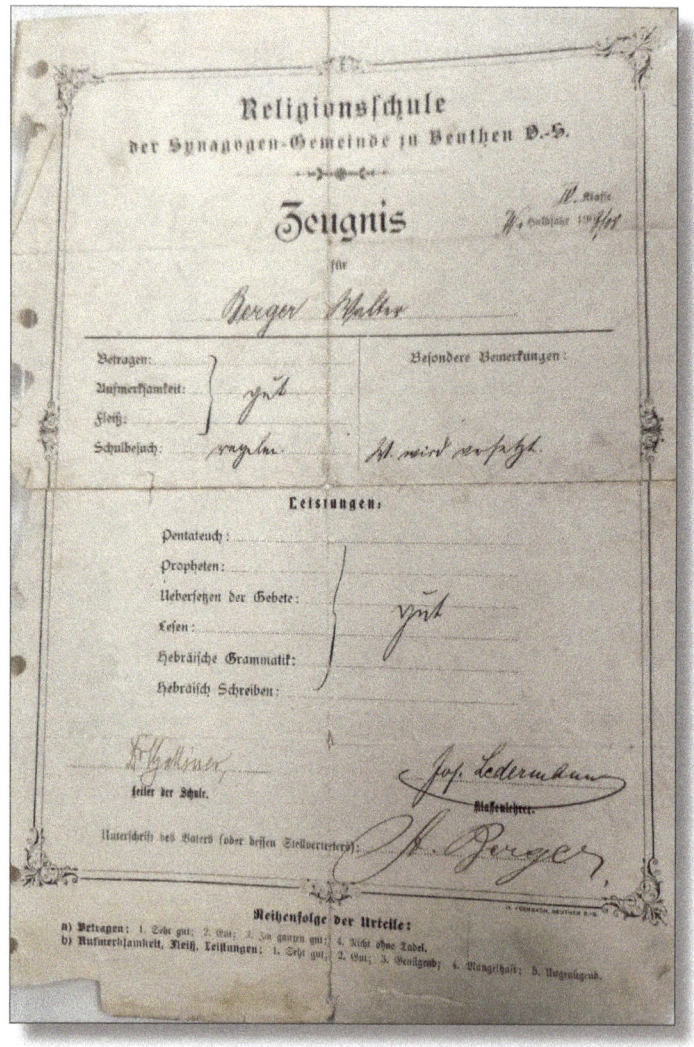

Report Card (Zeugnis) for Religious School, indicating good understanding of reading and writing in Hebrew.

About Me

My two older brothers, Max and Julius, were good in school too, but in general they were a little more carefree. They were regular guys who worked in the family store and enjoyed themselves on their rare days off. I was studious—especially serious about math, business, and music. My brother Max and I took lessons at a local music school. We both took piano, and I also learned to play the violin. Later, when we three boys worked full-time at the store, I was the one who maintained the books, even though I was the youngest. I found I was good with details, which came in handy both at the store and later in life—when pursuing paths leading to safety and security required careful attention to detail. For many years Max, Julius, and I worked in the store, which was originally named for my father and his brothers and later passed down to us three boys. Our sisters, Henriette, Ernestine, and Elfrieda, worked there for a while too, but ultimately moved away to live their own lives in various places in Germany. I'm sorry that I lost track of them, but in those days, young people grew up, got married, and often moved away. When we were all together as children, we were very close.

War and More

WHEN WORLD WAR ONE broke out, I couldn't wait to serve. I was proud of Germany—proud to be a German—and I wanted to do my part to defend my country. I enlisted in the army and served in a regiment of the cavalry from the time I was 20 years old (in 1916) until I was 22.

I kept a log of everything I did during the war, which included working with horses. One day, I was thrown from my horse while on duty, injuring my leg and causing my left knee to buckle. I was given precious little time to recover before returning to action and did so without proper treatment. As a result, I walked with a limp for the rest of my life. After the war was over, I tended the store with Max and Julius, thankful that my physical health was strong enough at least to do that work.

We sold a little bit of everything: linens, clothing and shoes, canned goods, tools, coal (which was vital in those days for heating homes), potatoes, onions, and pots and pans. But the world's economy was struggling. Inflation was on the rise in the 1930s after the Great Depression. We struggled to make the business thrive. We paid attention to balancing the books, even during the tough times of inflation when it was hard to value goods realistically. The whole world was in economic distress, and everyone felt it as they spent even more money on basic goods. But the responsibility for these tough economic times was never accurately shared or explained well—it became clear to us that the Jews were being held responsible for this misfortune. The Jewish people were blamed as the main reason that Germany lost so much prosperity following World War I. There was a mistaken belief that the Jewish people were twisting the economy behind the scenes to enrich only themselves. This blaming of Jews as greedy spoilers and thieves, who were trying to take over the world, was Nazi propaganda and was simply not true. While it was true that my family had a store and that we earned a living, we worked hard every day to make a go of it during the tough times of world inflation. We certainly were never rich, so it all sounded to me like a basic misunderstanding as well as a lie!

Inside the family store in Beuthen

Music and Marriage

I CAN'T REMEMBER A TIME when I didn't love music. I studied violin and piano in music school, and I felt most at home when I was practicing the violin or playing for other people. It was very big in Germany in those days to be able to play an instrument. Typical middle-class music-loving Germans were we!

Mozart was my favorite composer if I had to pick one. I loved to play for people, which because I was shy, also saved me from having to generate a lot of conversation. People loved my music, and sharing it felt good to me. For a few years, my routine was to work in the store and play music on the side for family and friends, but this stable and happy life was not to last. As the 1930s wore on, the skies were darkening in the country. By the middle of the decade, Europe was becoming visibly dangerous for Jewish people, with ever-increasing state-imposed restrictions.

The antisemitic, racist 1935 Nuremberg Laws that were enacted in Nazi Germany removed citizenship rights for all except those deemed eligible to be citizens of the Reich by virtue of their "racially pure" German blood. The rest of the population were subjects of the state without rights and were discriminated against at every turn. Such was the grim reality for Jewish people at this time.

Horrible and insulting as it was, we went about our business as best as we could. We all thought that as honorable Germans, everyone would come to their senses! We couldn't imagine that the treacherous madman Hitler and the Nazis would last long as the leaders of civilized Germany. After all, we were the land that produced Felix Mendelssohn, Thomas Mann, and Johann Wolfgang von Goethe—the most highly cultivated artistic figures known to the Western world came from Germany. We naively thought the political madness would blow over and that cooler heads would prevail.

Music and Marriage

That was the outside world. I was still a young man, and my personal hopes and dreams were coming to full flower. When I was in my early 30s, I was introduced to Else Grünberger from Ratibor, a nearby city that was also in the region of Upper Silesia. I was four years older than Else. Her family was also Jewish, and she came from an even larger family than me. Her six brothers were Lothar, Hans, Fritz, Jehuda, Ernst, and Kurt, and she had one sister, Ruth. Else was the sixth child born into her family of eight. When she was young, Else worked as a nanny and a household helper. She was gentle and quiet, so it wasn't easy for her to work demanding jobs full-time. Else possessed a delicate temperament—gentle and inclined to melancholy. She reminded me of the Romantic composer Robert Schumann with her brooding and her periods of depressive sadness. Even so, like the great composer Schumann, she worked hard and was successful. Else routinely received good job references, especially for taking care of children. We dated for a few years before we were married in the Beuthen Community Synagogue on December 23, 1935. In addition to my brother-in-law Yehuda Karmi, the congregation's president, Professor Dr. Ludwig Golinski, and Cantor Julius Tarschis officiated in both German and Yiddish.

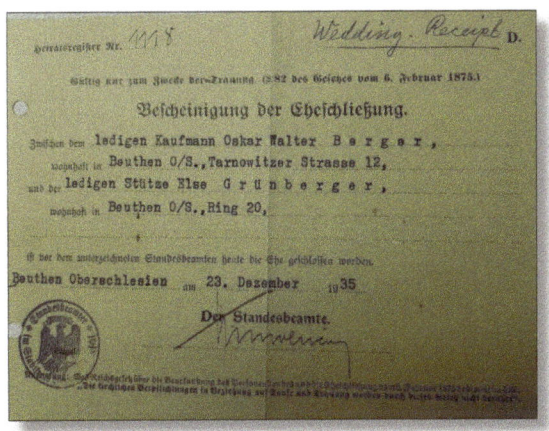

My Wedding Receipt and Marriage Certificate

We hoped that life in Germany would improve, that things would finally get better for the struggling economy and for the Jewish people in particular. As Jews, we were looking over our shoulder all the time now. Like everyone else, Else and I hoped for the best, but we were misguided in our belief. Even before 1935 and the imposition of the formalized Nuremberg Laws, we had known that Jewish people were no longer respected. I never fully grasped how the Nazis could consider Aryans the only good Germans—the only acceptable ones. We were racially discriminated against and blamed for all social ills. The Nuremberg Laws dictated what Jewish people could and could not do. For example, Jewish doctors and lawyers could only treat Jewish patients and clients, and Jewish children could only attend Jewish schools. All in all, Jewish people were considered inferior. This was always hard for me to understand because I, a proud veteran of the Great War, loved Germany as much as anyone and had defended my noble country. However, our beloved Germany had changed in menacing ways before our very eyes. We tried to be positive. What else could we do? I always believed you must do your best. I continued to work at the family store and Else continued to work as a homemaker and household helper. Now that we were getting older, we really wanted to have a baby. A year into our marriage, to our great sadness, Else delivered a stillborn daughter. Naturally, we were devastated, but we tried again—and when Else became pregnant a second time, we crossed our fingers and prayed. This time, the pregnancy went well.

Taken Away

Taken Away

OUR ENTHUSIASM WAS CUT short when I heard banging on the door early one morning in June 1938. Men from the Gestapo, the Nazi political police, came to the house looking for me, in what would be the first mass arrests of adult male Jews in Nazi Germany. I was arrested and taken away without any charges filed against me. I was arbitrarily considered to be a political prisoner—an enemy of the state. This was happening every day to Jewish men, and had it been a few years later, they would have taken my pregnant wife too. I was never told if the police suspected me of having done anything wrong in general, or anything against the government specifically. Maybe they suspected me of being a Communist, or maybe just my being Jewish was enough reason for them to put me in prison. Whatever the reason, the experience was terrifying. After being in jail for three days, I was sent to the Buchenwald concentration camp, where I was imprisoned for seven months, until December 1938. Poor Else was home alone preparing for the arrival of our baby, but I couldn't be with her. She must have been beside herself.

During that terrible time, I was always afraid. I saw people brutally beaten all around me. The guards made us work doing heavy physical labor. They forced me to dig rocks in the quarry, which was especially difficult for me because of my war injury, and I suffered constantly. Once I was so badly beaten around my neck that, for a long time, I couldn't even lift my head. Many years later, when I finally got medical care in America, the doctors told me that I shouldn't work anymore, and that I should be compensated by Germany for the abuse instigated by the guards in the prison camp. In later years I was awarded a small monthly pension from the German government, which they called "reparations", to compensate for such poor treatment under the Nazi regime.

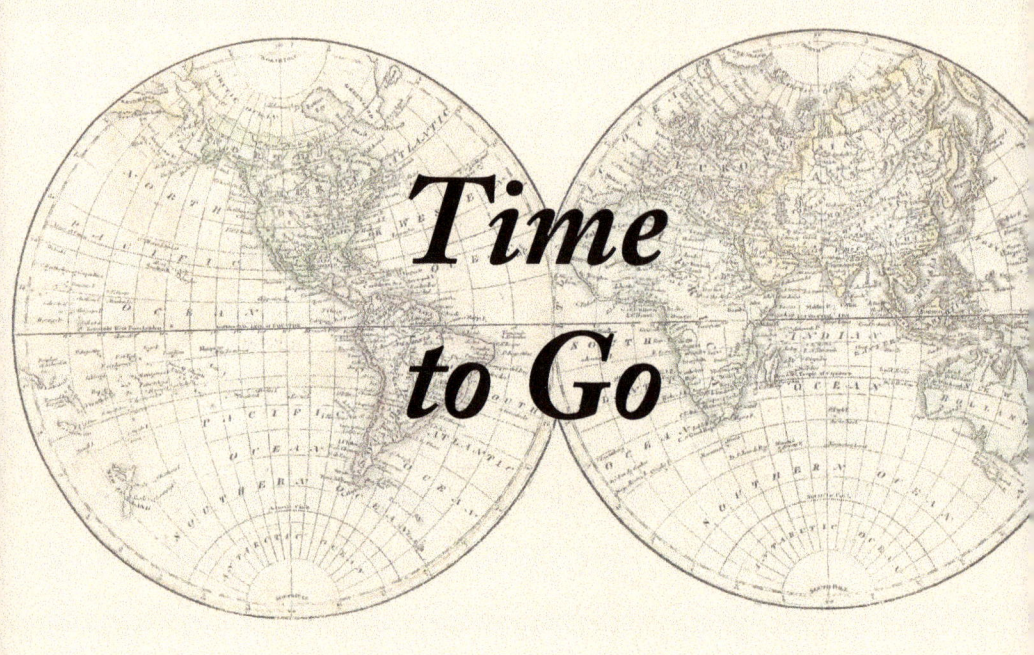

Time to Go

Time to Go

WHILE I WAS TRYING to survive in Buchenwald, Jewish-owned businesses all over Germany were being raided, looted, and outright taken over by the Nazis. Our beloved family store was one of the ones taken. I couldn't believe what was happening right here in my homeland! I learned later that my brothers were taken away, and the Nazis assumed ownership of the store without giving us any money for it. They stole everything.

While I was still in prison, Else gave birth to our beloved daughter, Gittel, born on October 27, 1938.

Less than two weeks after our little Gittel's birth, the nightmare we were living came to a climax when the Nazis committed the unspeakable crime known as Kristallnacht. The infamous "Night of Broken Glass" that occurred on November 9th and 10th of 1938 targeted all the Jewish businesses with destruction. Shards of broken glass littered the streets after the Nazis smashed the windows of Jewish-owned stores, buildings, homes, and synagogues during this

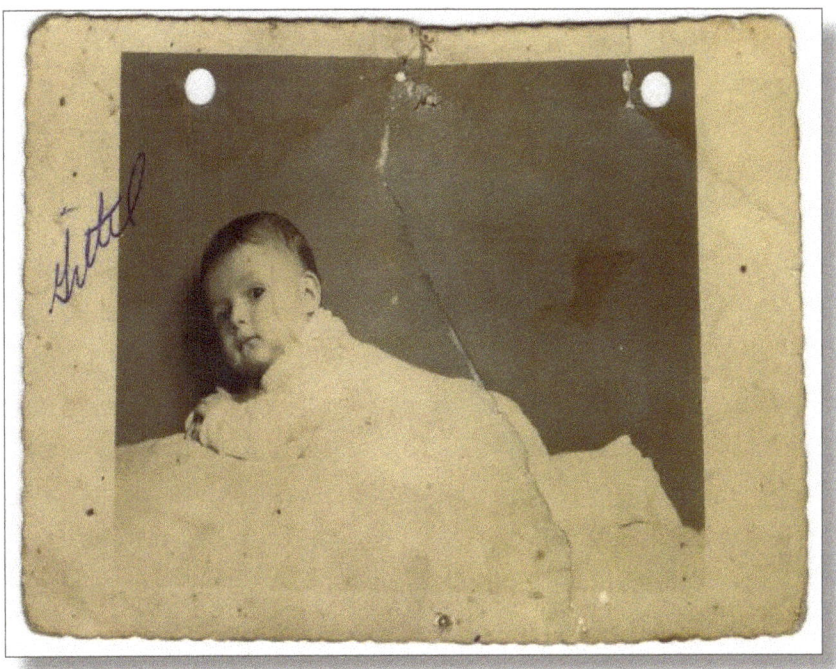

organized act of state-sanctioned violence and unrestrained antisemitism. We received our beautiful daughter into the world at the exact same time that Jewish lives were being ravaged—in that moment, the best and the worst things in my life came together.

One guard appreciated music, and spoke to me like a colleague because he also knew and loved Mozart and had heard I played the violin. He said that I would be released from Buchenwald if I agreed to leave the country immediately with my wife and daughter. I am forever grateful that he took me aside to warn me and give me instruction. All my life, music has sustained and nurtured me. At this critical juncture, in that act of kindness from a music-loving prison guard, I believe that music even saved my life.

Time to Go

Of course, I said I would do whatever they told me to do, and I was freed from Buchenwald on December 19, 1938, after seven terrifying months, with a pledge to leave the country.

Documentation of release from Buchenwald

29

Never Enough

I TOOK THEIR WORDS AS urgent, so I immediately looked for a way out for Else, the baby, and me. First, I contacted the Hilfsverein (Jewish Aid Agency) for assistance. Yehuda Karmi from the Beuthen Synagogue knew about the Hilfsverein and gave me the contact information.

Since 1912, Jews from around the world had helped each other by giving money to support first Russian, and then European Jews through this relief agency. Since we had lost the family business when the Nazis seized it, I really needed the advice and aid from the Hilfsverein. Else and I didn't have enough money to go anywhere.

With potential support coming now, I wrote to two of the possibilities for relocation that I had heard about—Bolivia (in South America) and Palestine (now called Israel). My letters to them were urgent appeals to admit us. Unfortunately, I was rejected by both countries. Bolivia's government said their country couldn't accept us because there were not even enough jobs for their own people and Palestine rejected us because I couldn't show that we had enough money in the bank to support ourselves. We needed to show that we had 1,000 Reichsmarks (about $20,000 today), which we didn't have.

I also had to obtain a police release, indicating that I was eligible to leave the country. Even though the Nazis wanted us gone, we had to go through the steps of demonstrating that we had no criminal records. Fortunately, I was able to secure that release document in the spring of 1939.

I was panicked and felt the walls were closing in on us. We had to leave Germany, but it was impossible to get a visa to go anywhere in the world—except Shanghai.

Flight to safety

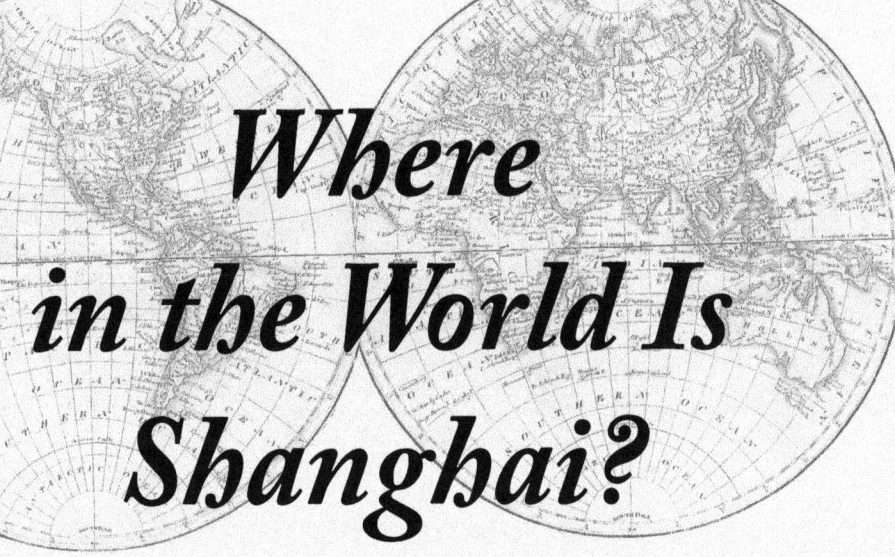

Where in the World Is Shanghai?

A Letter to My Family

THE PORT CITY OF Shanghai is in northeastern China, separated from the southernmost island of Japan by the East China Sea.

Like Hong Kong today, Shanghai was a busy harbor, exchanging merchandise from all around the world. For a long time, Shanghai did not impose restrictions on travelers coming and going so that merchants could do business freely. This openness was welcome news to European Jews, who were increasingly being denied entry to most other countries in the world. Whether the United States, South America, England, or Palestine—countries closed their borders to average (non-wealthy) Jewish people through rigid and narrow quotas. In the decade following the Great Depression, no country dared to offer opportunities to refugees who lacked the resources to sustain themselves. Most German Jews desperately needed to leave the country, but finding a place where they would be welcome was increasingly difficult without a visa. Forced out with nowhere to go, millions became known as Displaced Persons (DP). Shanghai was the port of last resort for banished people with no money. Around 16,000 European Jews flocked to Shanghai through the summer of 1939 in a "panic migration," but then Shanghai proclaimed itself filled to capacity and closed its doors as well (Hochstadt, p. 4).

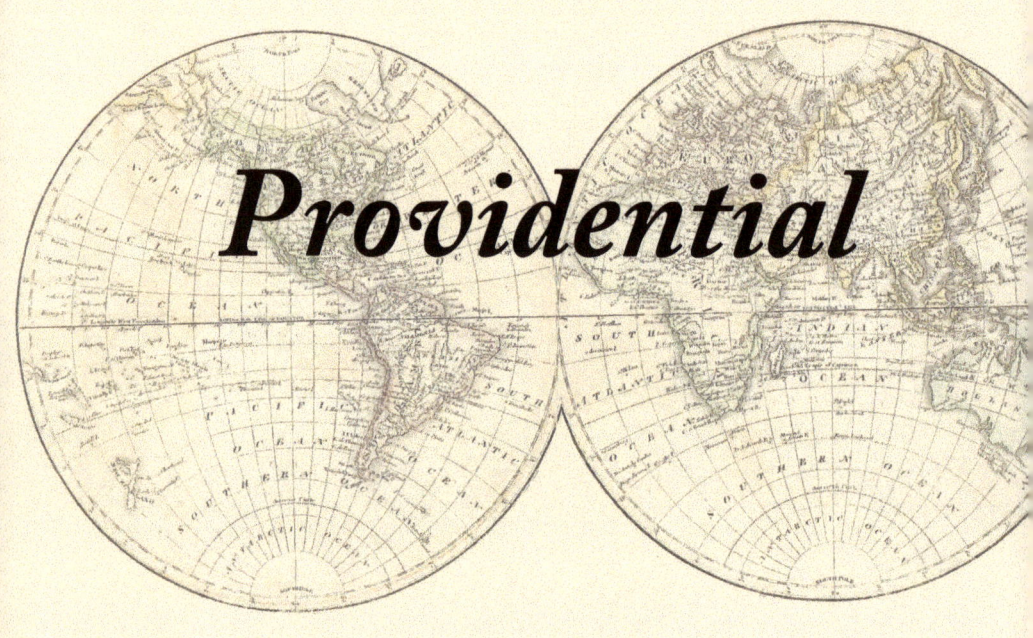

Providential

Providential

ONLY BY GOOD LUCK were Else and I able to buy tickets to Shanghai in April and May of 1939, slipping in just under the wire. By late August 1939, only three months later, the doors to Shanghai that had once been so wide-open slammed shut. For us, by a miracle, it was not too late. Else, Gittel, and I made it out of Germany.

I went ahead to Shanghai to find out what we could expect. With funds from the Hilfsverein, I was able to buy a ticket for myself to travel April 20, 1939 (ironically, Hitler's 50th birthday). People were no longer permitted to take money out of the country, so any cash we raised could only be used for travel. The Nazis wanted us gone without any equity that could be used to enrich our lives or be used against them.

I was dazzled by the big ship. Growing up in Germany, I had never even heard of Shanghai, and now I found myself enroute to the exotic land to escape the horrible things that were happening to me and everyone I knew. Culturally, Shanghai really was the end of the world. As a European, England would have had more of a familiar feel to it, but with no further options, I set out for the far reaches of Asia. I caught a cargo train from Germany south into northern Italy and in Genoa, thanks to my paid ticket, I boarded the biggest ship I've ever seen. The ship filled up completely and we set out.

A Letter to My Family

The Long Journey

First, we headed east. The route took us through the Suez Canal, across the Arabian Sea, past the southernmost tip of India, and we stopped to refuel in Colombo, Sri Lanka (my passport shows a stamp for this pause). Continuing east, the ship passed Thailand and then headed north, sailing along the shore between Hong Kong and Taiwan. Finally, a month after we left Italy, we arrived in Shanghai. I wrote to Else that she should follow. Fortunately, one of Else's cousins had set up a fund to raise the additional cash needed for Else's ticket, and a month later in May, she and seven-month-old Gittel took the exact same voyage. I stayed in temporary quarters, like a base camp, until they arrived. While I waited, I looked for a job and a place for us to live in that jam-packed city so far from home.

Living in the Jewish District

A Letter to My Family

ELSE JOINED ME IN Shanghai with 7-month-old Gittel in May 1939. We experienced severe culture shock at suddenly finding ourselves in China. As unfamiliar and remote as Shanghai was to me as a German-speaking European merchant, I was thankful for the thousands of other Jewish refugees that had arrived before me and paved the way. I was particularly grateful for an area called Hongkew, which was an established district that accommodated many people like us—families who had lost everything and had been forced out of their known world of Germany. Hongkew was called the Jewish district because so many European Jews lived there. After Japan became the dominant military power in Shanghai during the late 1930s, a formal Designated Area, already informally known as The Jewish Ghetto, was established by Japan in this area specifically for Jewish refugees. (Hochstadt, p. 77)

I quickly learned that we Europeans were not the only ones here—thousands of Baghdadi and Russian emigrants who were also Jewish were here too. We were all living together.

Crowded Housing in Hongkew (The Jewish District)

Living in the Jewish District

Between the unfamiliar surroundings, the strange language, and the huge numbers of new people and customs to learn, starting life again in China was not easy. We were crowded together, and many families lived together in dormitory-style housing. People slept in row after row of bunk beds and cooked in a common kitchen. I noticed unfamiliar smells and sounds as people prepared diverse foods and spoke different languages. Else and I were disoriented and distressed in this new world. While we were at least sheltered for now, we never felt secure. After having been such a proud businessman back home, my quality of life had rapidly spiraled downward. Gittel grew from a baby into a toddler. Young as she was, Gittel blessedly didn't really know what was going on or the distress we were in. Thankfully, she had both of her parents with her and knew she was loved. When she was old enough, she played with other refugee children and with a few Chinese children who lived nearby. The weather was perilous. In the winters the bitter cold was bone-chilling, and in the monsoon season water poured down from the heavens. Our section of the city had no sewer system, so water flooded the streets, taking everything with it—dead dogs, cats, rats—all floating in dirty water. I gave Gittel a metal tub and she charged friends a penny each to carry them across the street during the monsoon season so they didn't get their feet wet in the foul water…or float away themselves.

I found manual labor on a team of Chinese road workers, but the job paid very little. To say I had changed occupations was an understatement. I had gone from being a relatively bourgeois shop owner to working as part of a minimum-wage highway crew. Physical labor was always difficult for me because of my wartime injuries and the abuse at Buchenwald. I was now in my mid-40s and frail, but I had to persevere for the sake of our survival. With significant effort, I learned enough Chinese to get by. We were always anxious about money. On two separate occasions, I solicited a dentist to pull out a capped tooth so I could sell the gold filling to give us a little more income. One gold tooth at a time, these fillings provided a sliver of extra money so we could afford essentials.

All this while, Else and I tried to provide a normal childhood for Gittel. My beloved wife's health was always precarious. She was tired and sad most of the time, delicate and despondent even in the best of times. I wished I could have known what really ailed her. It was all I could do at the time to be supportive. I was the one who ventured out from the crowded apartment with Gittel for some fresh air and runs to the market. Some of the memories of those days were not good, including our witnessing Japanese soldiers barking orders and committing vicious cruelties in the streets. While the Western world was fighting for economic superiority among nations, China and Japan were feuding over military supremacy. In Shanghai, the conflict wasn't only because of the European war going on at the time—the Japanese and Chinese fought too. I did my best to shield our child from the threats all around her.

A Letter to My Family

FRIENDS WERE HARD TO come by at that time, so I really relied on news from home to find out about current conditions. In the days before computers and social media, postcards and letters were all we had to stay in touch. Luckily, we could receive mail at the Central Post Office in Shanghai. Else and I hung on to every word from home. We thought, if we heard from people at all, we would at least know they were still alive. I kept every card and letter we ever received, like this one from Max. I was amazed to see from the postmark that the mail came to us via Siberia—each postcard traveled by train entirely across Russia on its way to us in Shanghai. Everyone and everything were on a long-distance journey.

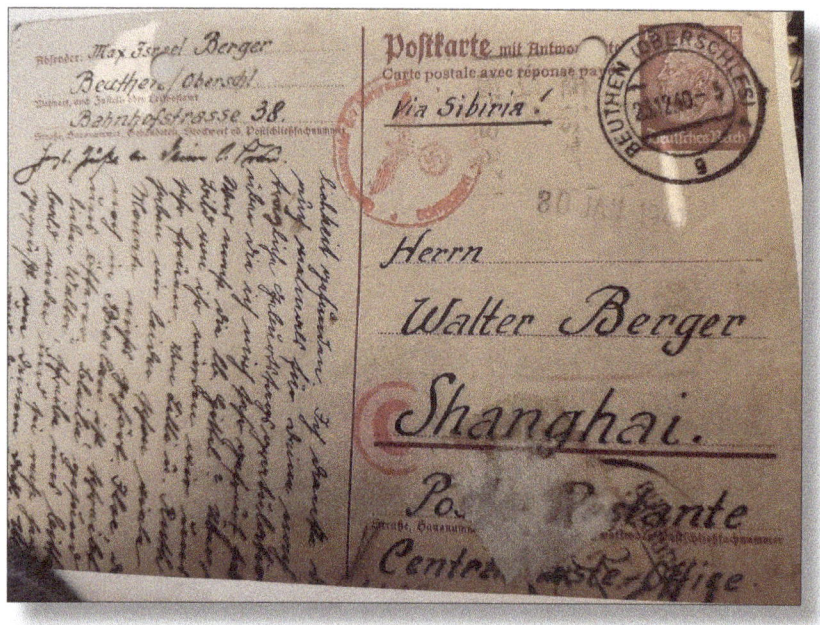

Postcard from Max in Germany to us in China

Home Fires Are Burning

WHILE ELSE AND I were in Shanghai trying to ride out the war and safeguard Gittel, the world was on fire back home. Unbeknownst to us at the time, Beuthen/Upper Silesia was in grave peril. Silesia turned out to be one of the first areas of Germany that the Nazis targeted once they had committed to their diabolical plan to rid the country of all its Jewish inhabitants in the early 1940s. Dreadfully called "The Final Solution," the German government's plan distorted itself from simply relocating the Jewish population (pushing them ever farther east) to complete elimination. "*Deutschland ist judenfrei*" ("free of Jews") was the Nazis' ghastly goal. By 1941, concentration camps such as Buchenwald, where I had been held for that terrible time as a political prisoner, were transformed into extermination camps. We later learned with horror that Upper Silesia comprised the first group of human souls gassed in Auschwitz in 1942. Now that I think about it, the scarce notes and cards that I ever got from Max along with the fact that I received nothing at all from Julius suggested the worst—that my dear brothers and sisters must have perished in the death camps. No Bergers were found after the war, so we never knew what happened to everyone.

Some family on Else's side still lived in Germany for a while and wrote to us. It wasn't easy for them either. I have correspondence from Louis Grünberger, Else's cousin, who practiced law until the Nuremberg laws prohibited German Jews from doing professional work. Louis wrote to us that the number of Jewish people still in Beuthen had diminished dramatically. The persecuted didn't all leave Germany at the same exact moment, but each left as soon as possible, working it out as they could for themselves. Everyone's story is unique. Over the years, people were scattered everywhere. Else had cousins who emigrated to South America, England, and Canada. Louis, for example, made it all the way to Toronto. After the war, he set up a law practice, which is what he would have been doing had the dreadful Nazi nightmare never occurred.

I wrote to all my remaining friends and contacts asking for suggestions on how to connect after the war. Else and I wanted desperately to get home and to provide Gittel a care-free childhood. I sent letters all around asking to be remembered when opportunities might arise after the conflict stopped. We knew that it was too soon to return to Europe. I tried to keep in touch with Else's cousins, but in the midst of the chaos, it was increasingly difficult to do so. Our desperation mounted. I tried to take heart and remember that the fighting had to stop someday. Every war ends eventually. We had to hang on.

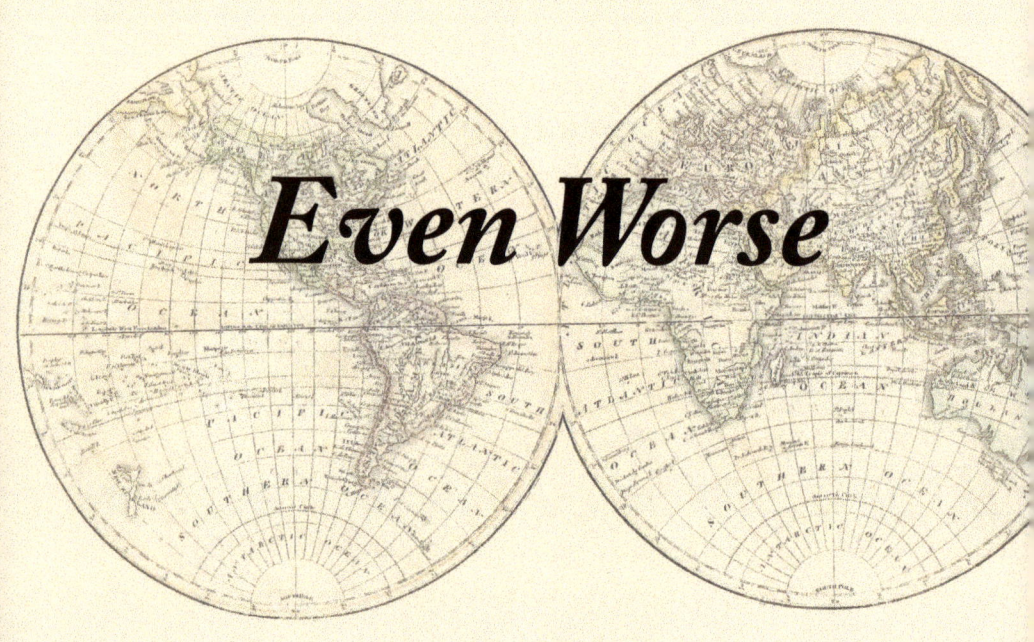

Even Worse

Even Worse

NEAR THE END OF the war our lives crashed again. As the fighting kept building in the Pacific, America lashed out against Japan, which was aligned with Germany. The Japanese had become too powerful and were taking over Shanghai. The United States decided to strike out against Japan, after their vicious attack on Pearl Harbor in 1941.

American planes bombed a radio tower on July 17, 1945, in an effort to cripple the Japanese stronghold. Unfortunately, this location sat dangerously near the Hongkew district where we and so many other refugees lived. While the radio tower was destroyed, 24 residents of Hongkew accidentally perished—including my beloved Else.

A Letter to My Family

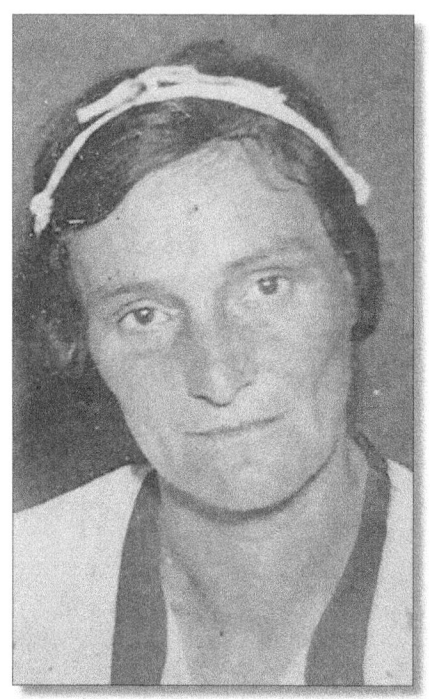

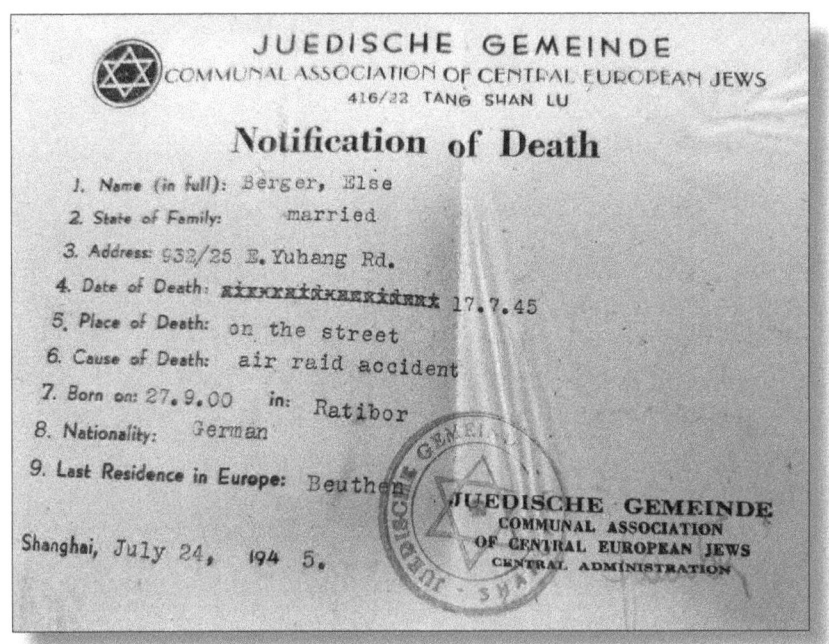

Death Notices for Else Berger, July 1945 in Shanghai

Else was 45 years old, and our lives together had only just begun. Gittel was only 6 years old. We had such high hopes, and now my dear wife was gone. My entire world collapsed. Still in shock, I had Else buried in the cemetery in the Jewish district. I pleaded with the American Jewish Joint Distribution Committee for funds to purchase a tombstone for my beloved wife but was unsuccessful. Known as "the Joint," the multi-national relief organization was founded in 1914 to assist persecuted European Jews. Based in New York, the Joint kept offices worldwide. The Joint cited its extremely limited funds and indicated that, while it was "warmly sympathetic," it was unable to grant the request for a tombstone.

Less than a month later, the war was finally over. In its aftermath, millions lay dead in Europe and the Pacific. In Shanghai, one middle-aged man remained who was now a widower with a young child who no longer had a mother.

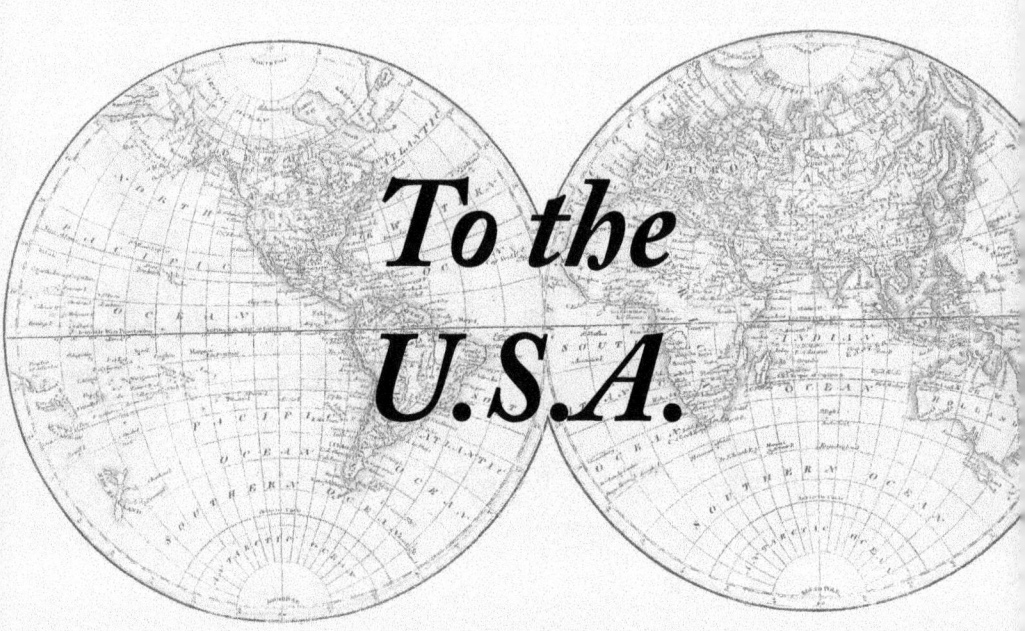

To the U.S.A.

To the U.S.A

As DISPLACED PERSONS, GITTEL and I were stateless—we had no country to claim officially as our home. After the war ended, we spent two more years in Shanghai before we were able to buy tickets to America with relief provided by the Joint. Tens of thousands more would come to the United States after the passing of the Displaced Persons Act (DPA), which allowed the established quotas to be overridden. The naval ship Marine Lynx, with Gittel and me on board, set sail for San Francisco on October 23, 1947.

The U.S. Naval Ship Marine Lynx

A Letter to My Family

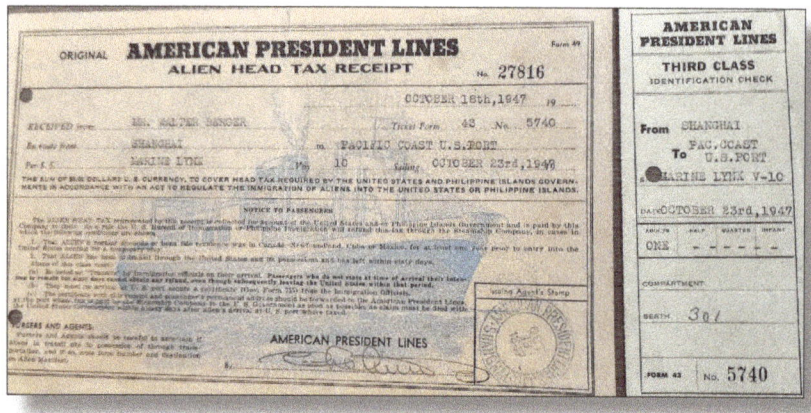

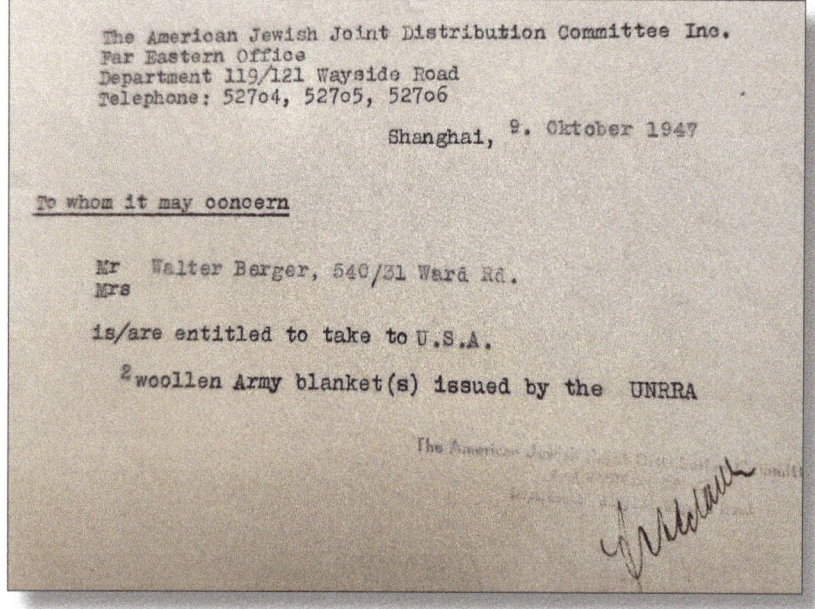

Gittel was excited to be leaving grim Shanghai and the Jewish ghetto and remembers fondly the kindness of the American naval personnel on board the ship. They played games with her, hoisted her on their shoulders, and four days into the voyage they gave Gittel her first American chocolate—a Hershey's bar—for her 9th birthday. It took a month to make our way across the Pacific Ocean.

Once we arrived in San Francisco, I researched our options with assistance from the relief organizations. Given the recommendation of three cities to move to, I chose St. Louis in hopes of finding a job there. Gittel excitedly rode the train from California to Missouri. She looked out the window at our beautiful new country as we rolled along through the American West. However, we were devastated to learn that the steamer trunk containing our few precious possessions and our only remaining memories of Else had been either lost or stolen on the way. We arrived in St. Louis with only one suitcase between us and my violin. Fortuitously, I brought the briefcase that contained all the correspondence I had saved over the years on the train with us.

We arrived in St. Louis the last week of May 1948. We took a small second-floor apartment downtown and began the task of establishing ourselves as residents of the United States. I looked for work and Gittel started school, where she learned English.

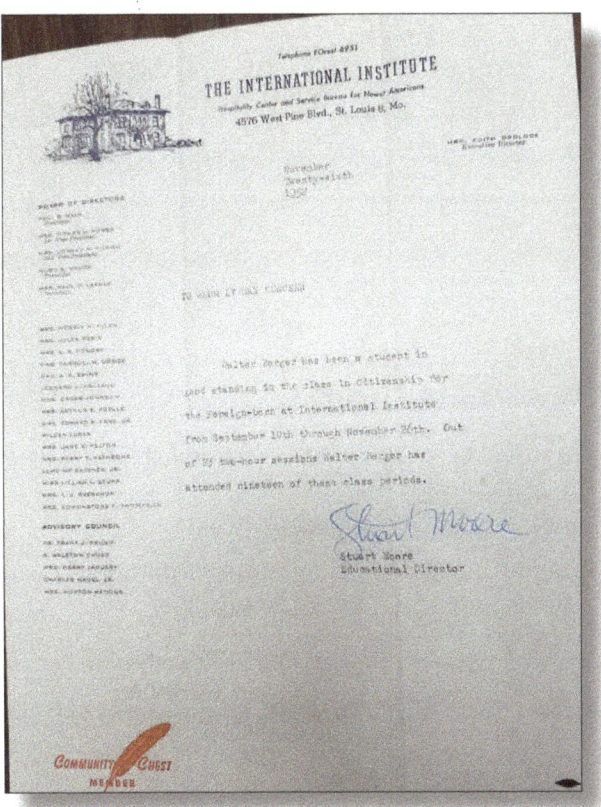

A Letter to My Family

I enrolled in evening courses at the International Institute, where I also studied English and prepared for a citizenship exam. I wrote to the International Red Cross to learn the whereabouts of family members, especially my brother Julius, because I had never once heard from him. Over the next several years, the Red Cross was not able to locate any of my siblings—not one.

This was the greatest pain, to know that once there had lived so many of us but now we were so few.

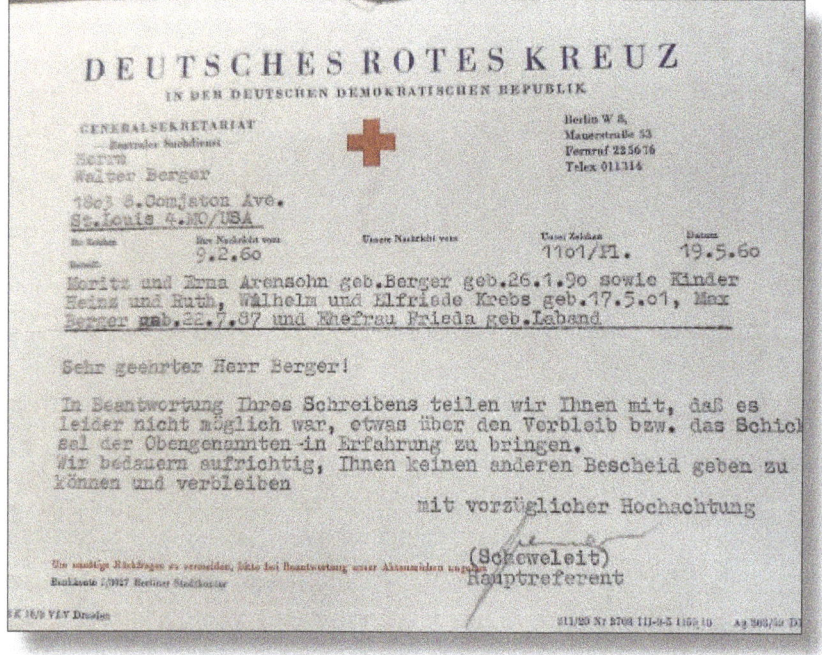

The German Red Cross can't locate anyone from Walter Berger's family.

Soon after we arrived, I came down with a bad case of the flu and needed to go into the hospital. We didn't know anyone in St. Louis, so Gittel was sent to stay in The Jewish Children's Home. A month later, I had fully recovered, and was discharged from the hospital. When I went to pick up Gittel, I was told that Child

Services had decided to keep her out of the house entirely, saying that I was a bad father and that Gittel needed a more secure home. After all that we had been through, I was both furious and distraught to have to fight for my daughter—the only person left in the world who meant anything to me.

A Letter to My Family

Involved In Custody Fight

A FIGHT for the custody of Gittle Berger, motherless 9-year-old refugee who arrived here from Shanghai last December, was on today between her father, Walter Berger (right) and the Jewish Family Service Agency. This picture of the youngster, now at the Jewish Children's Home, was made shortly after she and Berger came here.

Rain During Day, Night 1.09 Inches; Some Hail Falls

Scowling clouds dumped 1.09 inches of water on St. Louis from yesterday morning to noon today.

The wetness ranged from light showers to drenching downpours.

Refugee Widower Fighting Agency For Daughter, 9

A refugee widower is fighting a St. Louis welfare agency today for the custody of his 9-year-old daughter, who came to St. Louis with him from Shanghai last December.

To the U.S.A

News of the case of a displaced war widower fighting to keep his only child was published in newspapers like the St. Louis Globe Democrat. Thankfully, I was ultimately successful and reclaimed my daughter. Having attracted local press coverage, the story also caught the attention of a German family in nearby Illinois, who reached out to us in kindness and sympathy. Linda and Henry

Makler of Staunton befriended us—they welcomed us to spend weekends with them in the country. While Gittel and I lived in St. Louis City, we spent all our free time and holidays with the German-speaking Maklers, and we remained lifelong friends. It was such a relief to be able to speak my native language again! I could finally relax around other Germans after so many years struggling with Chinese and English.

After a few years of hard work learning American customs, laws, and language, I passed my citizenship course and was naturalized on December 4, 1953, at age 57. Gittel became a U.S. citizen in 1954 when she was 15. I found odd jobs, including working as a cemetery worker and as a baker's helper. My most meaningful pursuit was attending synagogue in the St. Louis's Central West End. I wanted to stay faithful to the Jewish customs I knew from my childhood—especially customs that I had seen observed by my father. I still remember Gittel lighting the Shabbat candles on Friday evenings on our tiny dining room table. I made a prayer corner in every apartment in which we lived and I rode a streetcar to services every Saturday in University City. I made some friends in St. Louis, and we spoke German and Yiddish together when we visited—I had a close-knit circle of friends (though I never learned to play cards). My Judaism sustained me always. I often said, "Hitler's era wanted to take the Jew out of me, but that is never going to happen."

Although I made the most of my new life in America, I could never really talk about the war or all that I had been through. A person can take just so much, and I had seen a great deal.

I played the piano and violin at family functions and enjoyed attending performances at the Muny Municipal Opera, which was St. Louis's outdoor theater. The blessings of music! I took the bus to travel around town. I enjoyed the actress (and swimmer) Esther

To the U.S.A

Williams and watched any show she appeared in. Life was acceptable for me now, however, I would forever feel ill at ease that I could never locate anyone from my side of the family. Most family on Else's side had been deported, though a few successfully emigrated. I tried to stay in touch, but our connections grew dim as the years went by. Everyone had been shattered by war. It wasn't within everybody's capacity to keep in touch even if they had wanted to.

I ask you—how can you be 50 years old, in the middle of life, and start over again and again? At times, life pushed me to the breaking point, but my daughter and I were here now and needed to make a life somehow.

In time, Gittel went on with her life and brought her own family into the world, out in Staunton. I remained in St. Louis and enjoyed living in my small city apartment, where I could follow my own path, whatever it was to be. In addition to attending services and listening to live music when I could, I followed the news. I was captivated by the 1961 Israeli trial and hanging of Nazi war criminal Adolf Eichmann. I kept a scrapbook with all the newspaper clippings about it, which was later also donated to the St. Louis Holocaust Museum. Most of all, in my remaining 13 years I was grateful to get to know two grandchildren, Cindy (whom I called "Cindy-boo") and her little brother Frank—both gave me such happiness. I enjoyed bringing them chocolate bars and toys when I visited.

Toward the Future

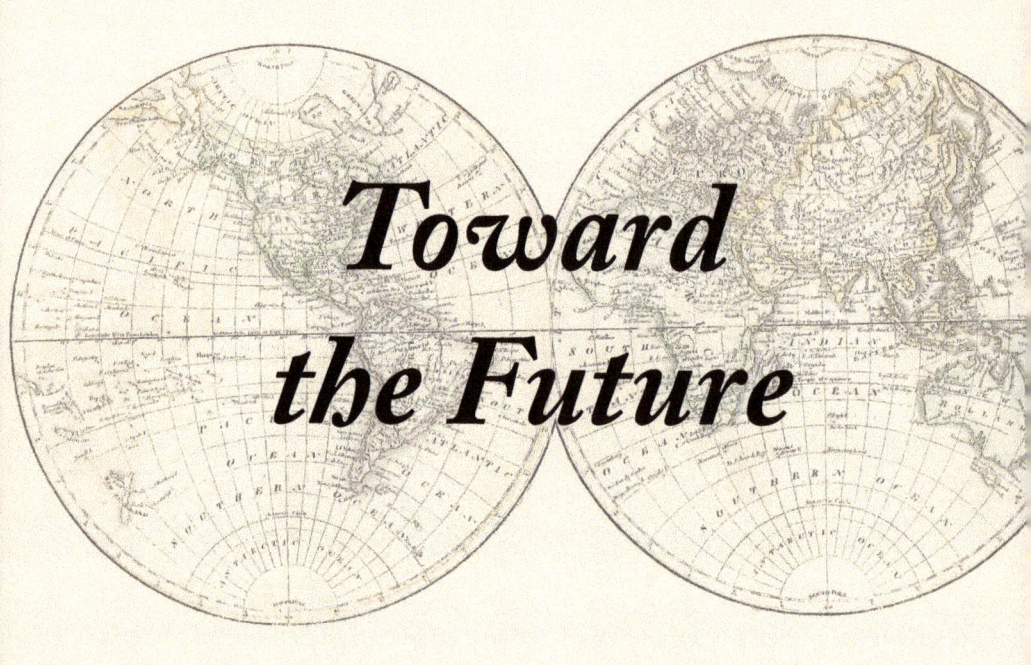

Toward the Future

LOOKING DOWN NOW FROM Heaven, I am thrilled that new generations are still being born to our family. I am happy to hear it, even though I have been gone now for some time. I am still so proud of Gittel. I think life was hard for her and I wanted to give her much more, but she has done so well. Mostly I am sad that Else died so young that Gittel never really knew her mother. I wish I could tell Gittel now that her mother always loved her, as do I, and that she never disappointed me. But we can only look forward. I was pleased to hear that family newcomer Grant Oscar carries with him my first name, too. Don't you agree that he looks a little bit like me?

Baby Grant Oscar and Oskar Walter

Now you have heard our immigration story, my beloved family.

Please know and remember that I always had my family first in my heart. Carry on and just do your best! We can't control much in this world, but we can decide how to respond to whatever comes our way.

Oskar Walter Berger

DATES OF WALTER'S STORY

10,000 Jews sent to Buchenwald prison camp, including Walter (June) Kristallnacht (November) two-day campaign against Jews	**1938**	Gittel born in Beuthen, Germany (October) Walter is released from Buchenwald (December)
The Bergers flee to Shanghai	**1939**	
Germany declares war on the United States	**1941**	Japan attacks Pearl Harbor (December) The U.S. declares war on Japan
The Nazi "Final Solution" master plan decided at Wannsee Conference (January) Concentration camps become killing centers	**1942**	The Bergers, in Shanghai, hang on for any news from home
D-Day (June)	**1944**	
Hitler commits suicide in bunker (April) Germany surrenders (May)	**1945**	Else dies in U.S. bombing in Shanghai (July) Japan surrenders (September)
Water and Gittel emigrate to the U.S.A.	**1947**	

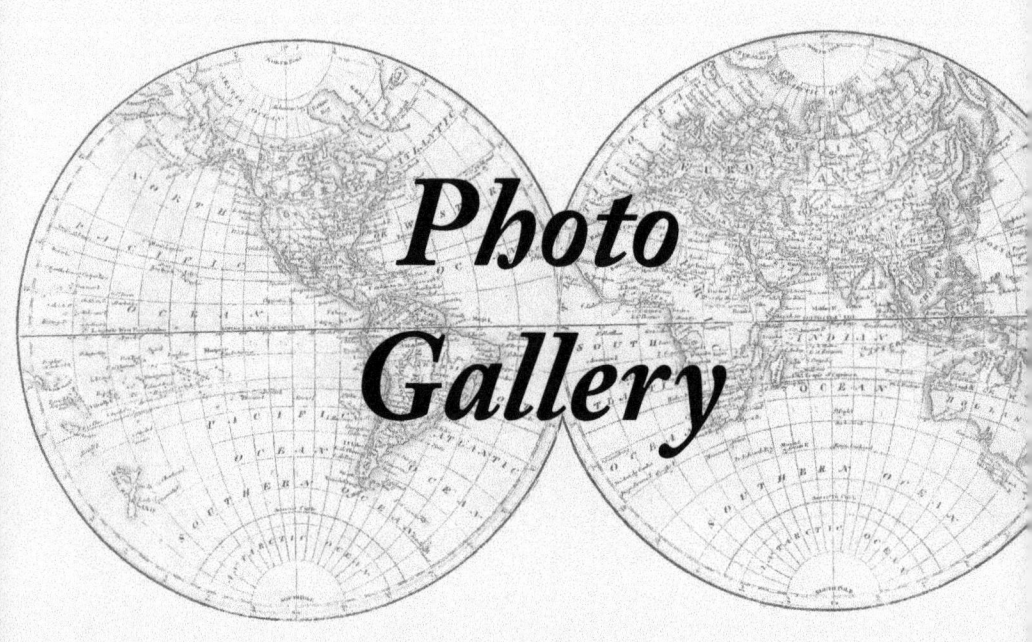

Photo Gallery

The St. Louis Kaplan Feldman Holocaust Museum re-opened in an expanded version in 2022 and relays the Berger story of flight among its permanent exhibits.

Gittel honors her father's likeness in the museum at the re-opening, November 22, 2022.

67

Gittel was interviewed for TV at the new museum re-opening November 22, 2022. She stands in front of the two letters showing how Walter was denied access to Bolivia and Palestine.

Photo Gallery

The two grandchildren Walter lived to know: Cindy and Frank
in front of his photo in the Museum, in 2022.

Walter, Gittel, and his grandchildren Cindy and Frank in 1963.

Photo Gallery

Walter's name is commemorated in a paver outside the new St. Louis Kaplan Feldman Holocaust Museum.

Walter Berger tat sein Bestes -- "Walter Berger did his best"

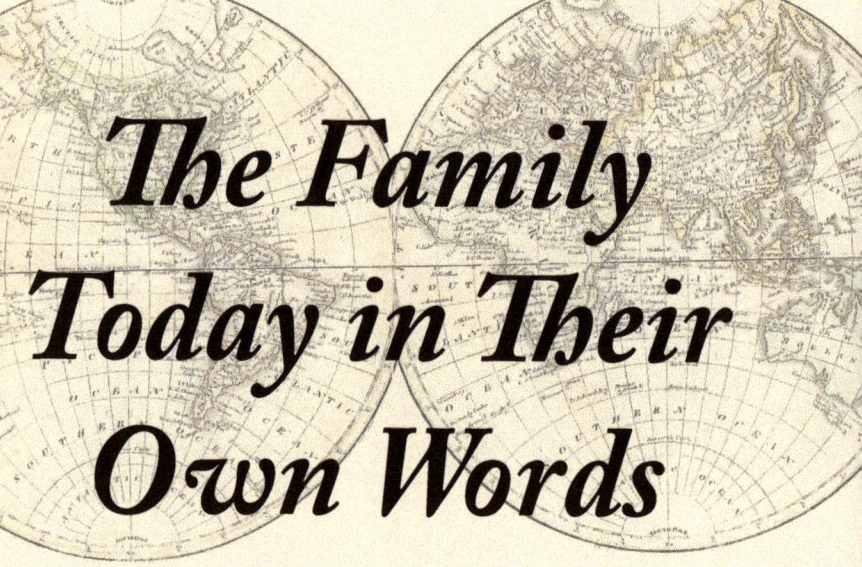

The Family Today in Their Own Words

The Family Today in Their Own Words

Gittel and her children (from left) Frank, Cindy, and Angie at the Museum in front of the interactive Berger permanent exhibit.

CINDY:

"As the oldest of the grandchildren, I have the benefit of vivid memories of my grandfather, Walter Berger. I always knew that both my mom and grandpa had suffered. But for years, no one spoke of it. Grandpa always put on a proud face. I remember sitting on grandpa's lap so we could read my German children's books. I sat next to him at the piano when he played. Though we always had a good time, at all times I sensed a sadness in my pawpaw. Even as a child, he seemed to me to be a broken man. I never knew why. I remember this lovely man who was just my gentle grandpa! I was eight years old when he died. I am pleased that he enjoyed his last years, and that he could know that his family and the next generations were safe in his adopted country. I also knew mom had been through a lot, but I never knew the extent of her experience until a few years ago. She kept a lot hidden while raising us kids and working. Mom treated everyone with respect and kindness, which she instilled in us. When she finally shared her story with us, she realized it was time to share it with the world. As Gittel says and I know for myself, this tragedy should not happen again!"

FRANK:

"Even when I was a teenager, I knew my Mom had been through some rough times. But I did not know the extent of it until she agreed to share her experience with the Holocaust Museum. I have learned so much more! Even with all the things she has seen and been through, Mom has always been a loving and caring person not only to family and friends, but to strangers as well. I am very proud of my Mom."

The Family Today in Their Own Words

ANGIE:

"My Mom never really spoke of the suffering she and her father endured. It was not until she began to share her story with the Holocaust Museum that I truly understood this history. My Mom is a survivor in so many ways and I am so thankful that our family's story is being shared with others, not only to continue to document this history, but to honor the memories of all those that suffered during this horrific time."

Gittel and Cindy at the St. Louis Holocaust Museum in 2022.

Gittel in 2022

Gittel's Epilogue: July 2023

A Letter to My Family

"The Holocaust should never be forgotten. I lived part of this history."

WHEN I THINK ABOUT it, I am relieved that my dad finally had some good years at the end of this wild journey—surviving Buchenwald, escaping from Nazi Germany, living as a refugee in Shanghai, losing his wife (and my mother) Else, and finally becoming a citizen and settling in the United States. Toward the end of his life (even at 68, he died far too young), my papa enjoyed living in St. Louis with his odd jobs and a small pension from the German government. He enjoyed playing piano and violin, and most of all, visiting his daughter (me!) and his precious grandchildren out here in Staunton. He was rightfully proud of having achieved citizenship in the United States. It was the start of a new life in a safe place. At the same time, it pains me to think that he lived the rest of his days after the end of the war looking for his beloved family, especially his two brothers, Julius and Max. The lives of all of them would have taken an entirely different turn if the Nazis had never come to power and stolen everything from them. For one thing, they all could have continued living happily in Beuthen, running the family business. Most of all, my mother would have lived to grow old with my father, and I would have had a chance to really know her. Instead, our lives were marked by trauma with the displacement from Germany to Shanghai following the loss of everything back home. And my dear Mama didn't live long enough to see America.

Thinking about my family's story makes me very sympathetic to others' stories. I can't imagine what all the other refugees went through—it wasn't just us. The awful day that my mother died in the bombing in Shanghai, many other women were also killed as well—and they all had families. We weren't the only ones.

Gittel's Epilogue: July 2023

I have now learned enough of this history to understand better than I did as a child. I see now that here in America, people were not always gracious to one another in the old days. For one thing, when my dad and I arrived in St. Louis, there weren't the social services available to us that are available now. My dad scrambled for work and really struggled to learn English. I was shuffled around from place to place and put to work in kitchens. I don't remember a lot of compassion or understanding for what we'd been through as displaced war refugees.

I do feel happy that I survived it all. I have wonderful kids, grandchildren, and even great-grandchildren. I suppose I am a little wiser now (finally!). As the saying goes, "Old too soon and wise too late."

But it's not too late to understand more about what my dad must have felt—he went through many hardships, but he never gave up. Sometimes I think that if he had had more time to learn English, he could have made something more of himself over here—but perhaps he had simply been through too much.

My dad was a proud man and delighted in his coal-black hair. Having always been slight of build and short of stature, he appreciated his full, thick, black head of hair. Not too long after we arrived in St. Louis, he suffered a small stroke and landed in the hospital. I went to see him for a while before saying good night and leaving him. The next day when I visited, I was shocked to see that overnight, every hair on his head had turned snow white. The hospital staff was hesitant to respond to his requests for a hand mirror—nobody wanted to see his reaction. When my papa finally saw himself in a mirror, he broke down and cried to see that his jet-black hair had suddenly lost all its color.

I wish I could have gotten to know Walter Berger better. He was my father, but I see now that he was a great person. I regret that

I didn't always appreciate him at the time. It was so hard to grow up without my mother and I took my angry feelings about losing her out on him. I blamed him for not helping guide me better as a girl and young woman growing up in America. But many years have gone by and now I think how it would have been wonderful if we could have taken Walter in to live with us—I had such a good marriage and could have provided a home—maybe even given back some of what he gave me.

When I speak at museums or other gatherings about my Holocaust experience, I am invariably asked for my "message". I say, we have to keep learning about what happened so that it can never happen again.

"War is hell on everybody. But we keep making war. When is it ever going to end?"

Presenting in 2018 to the United Hebrew Congregation in St. Louis.

Gittel's Epilogue: July 2023

Gittel presenting to granddaughter Molly's class
visiting the Holocaust Museum in 2023.

The Journey from Walter's Perspective

The Journey from Walter's Perspective

Walter and Gittel had to travel around the world to reach far-away America.

A family portrait in 2022. Gittel is holding the white dog.

Gittel and Frank visiting Water Berger's gravestone in Staunton, Illinois in 2023.

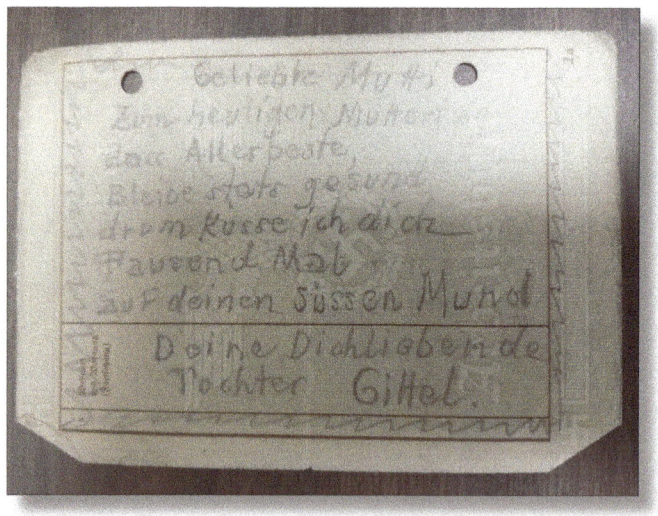

Gittel's first language was German, as seen in this undated Mother's Day card to Else (ca. 1945).

Little Gittel: 18 months old [ca. 1940].
The name "Gittel" appears in Else's family tree in 1845.

A Letter to My Family

German-language newspaper serving displaced
Jews in Shanghai during the war.

Walter and Gittel in St. Louis in 1949. Walter loved his cigars!

The Journey from Walter's Perspective

Walter's language book makes learning English fun for Germans.

A Letter to My Family

The Journey from Walter's Perspective

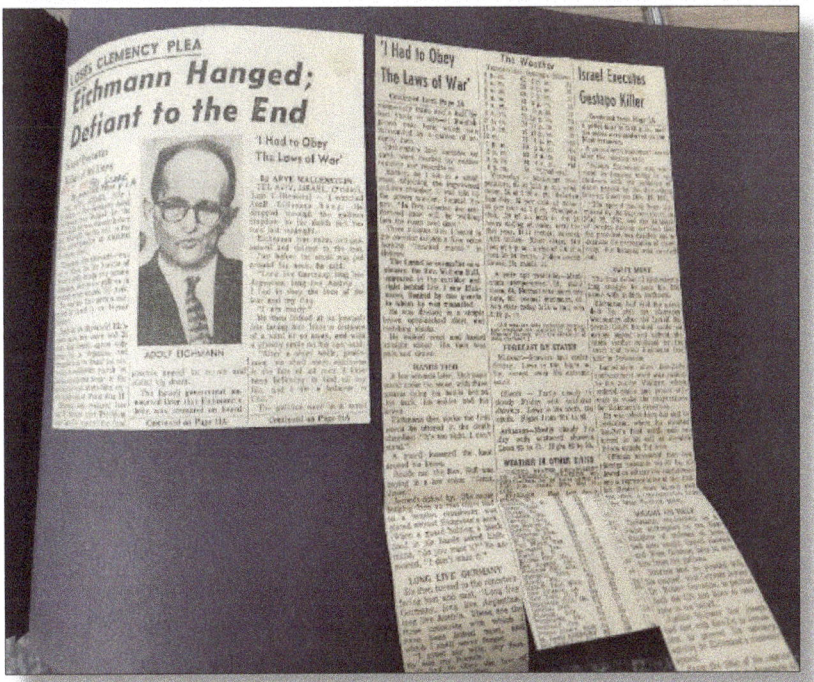

Walter filled scrapbook with articles about Nazi war criminal Adolf Eichmann's trial in Israel (1961).

A Letter to My Family

"Solitude" from 1933 is by the great Russian French artist Marc Chagall (1887-1985). The ominous dark sky and the city on fire in the background suggest how Walter might have described the turmoil in Europe in the 1930s. This religious man, clinging to the Torah scroll, is serenaded by a violin while an angel watches over.

Epilogue

Epilogue

HOW THIS BOOK CAME TO BE

In 2016, Gittel Burns and her daughter Cindy Schrage contacted the St. Louis Holocaust Museum and Learning Center.

They had in their possession a suitcase containing 300 letters and documents that had been saved by Gittel's father. It told his story of escaping to Shanghai during the Holocaust. Museum archivist, Diane Everman, and curator, Dan Reich, promptly met with them to hear the story and review the materials. That initial meeting began a robust and continuing relationship. As they sat down together and opened the briefcase, attention was swiftly focused on the story's central character.

Walter Berger had painstakingly saved every letter, photograph, note, postcard, receipt, ticket, certificate, and document from his early life in Germany all the way to his later years in St. Louis. Numerous letters and documents were preserved from his flight from Germany to Shanghai during the Holocaust. The Museum was honored to study and share this comprehensive collection that had been so carefully preserved through so many long journeys. In short order, Gittel's oral history was recorded, and the collection was processed. Cataloging involved Everman reviewing each item and organizing each one chronologically. The images and papers were placed in acid-free enclosures, each carefully labeled in pencil where identifications and dates were known.

The collection was a treasure trove in that it contained such a large quantity of primary source material so carefully preserved for half a century—despite being hauled over perilous paths. Almost all the documents were in German. Museum staff were well-versed in German because many artifacts and documents that regularly come to the Museum are *auf Deutsch*, so everyone there has a working knowledge of the language. But to have such a comprehensive

93

collection, almost all in German, of one family's expedition so carefully preserved—this was something new for staff to grasp and integrate.

The Archives department of the Museum has a 20+ year relationship with several German language programs in local universities. Diane Everman got in touch with Paula Hanssen, head of the German Department at Webster University, to see if a student might be interested in applying for an internship so that one person could be dedicated to the new collection full-time.

In early 2018, I had moved to St. Louis from New York City to study German language and culture. Having been involved in musical projects in Germany, I was interested in learning more about the country, and decided to return to college to pursue a formal degree program in German. At age 59, I was semi-retired following a 30-year career as a Broadway musician, university music professor and administrator. I enrolled as a degree student in the undergraduate German program at Webster University as what is considered a "non-traditional" student. My academic advisor, Dr. Paula Hanssen, suggested that I interview with Dr. Diane Everman, Archivist at the St. Louis Holocaust Museum and Learning Center. Happily, I was accepted as one of the museum's interns for 2018 and was assigned to the collection of Walter Berger's material.

My first thought upon seeing the collection was that 300 preserved items is a lot to wrap one's arms around, but I am good at organizing. I generated subcategories of everything for my own purposes so that I could orient myself within the collection. I created identifiers and established a "BB" numbering system, which classifies each item by a distinct number. "BB" in this case stands for Berger Burns, named for Walter Berger, but also for Gittel Burns. Gittel was the family's keeper of the collection in addition to being a child survivor herself. I organized materials by genre as

Epilogue

well as by time—all the official documents together and all the personal letters together. This method proved invaluable as I moved further into the collection and needed to keep things in order.

I also created new pages with BB call numbers and made a contact list of the family members discussed in the letters, their connection to Walter, their known or assumed whereabouts, and their place in the collection.

EXAMPLE: WALTER BERGER CONTACTS (EXCERPT)

BB20	Max and Frieda	Beuthen	Walter's brother and wife
BB20	Professor Golinsky	Palestine	Family acquaintance
BB20	Frieda	Breslau	Else and Max's aunt
BB22	Fritz	To Auschwitz	Else's brother
BB21	Hans Grünberger	Concentr. Camp	Else's brother. Wife is Edith; daughter Ilse (see 1960s)
BB30	Hedel	Beuthen	Aunt (Unknown which side)

I began by working with printed correspondence, then moved outward to the handwritten letters, which were quite daunting. There is a world of difference between translating a typed page such as a government-issued document and deciphering a handwritten letter. Historically, more than one font was used in German scripts, and on top of that, people's handwriting styles varied widely—just as they do today. Various handwriting styles were used by authors of letters to Walter.

Epilogue

Before standardization to a modern alphabet following WW II, handwriting in Germany featured different types of scripts.

A Letter to My Family

Epilogue

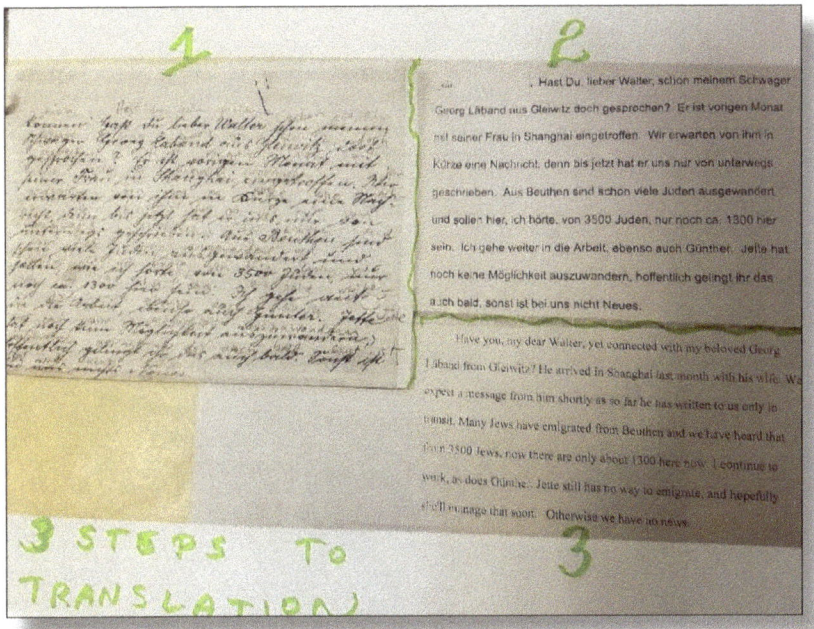

There are three steps to translate handwritten correspondence. The first is to pencil in modern German above a copy of the original cursive. Second, the Modern German must be typed out.

Finally, the correspondence can be typed out in English. The museum saves the both the German and English typed versions.

Lisa working on translations in consultation with
German Fulbright Scholar Malte Hansen (Webster University 2019).

Epilogue

Gittel reviewing translations in 2019.

AUTHOR'S NOTE

    Walter Berger kept all his paperwork, but unfortunately, a personal diary does not exist. Naturally, we would prefer to hear his thoughts and feelings in his own voice, but that is not possible. Nonetheless, an indirect account of Walter's experience IS possible. In living with the collection for several years now, I have discerned a distinct feeling for Walter Berger as an individual, which is why I call him "Walter." I endeavored to write this letter on his behalf. The images dispersed throughout come mostly from the collection and are woven together with narrative.

    A Letter to My Family summarizes what I discovered from the collection about Walter Berger—what came into my purview as Walter's "spirit" expressed itself through the assembly of items that he so lovingly preserved. I hope he would approve of my efforts in telling his story, but I know for sure that he would say, "You did your best and that is all anyone can do."

Lisa Johnson
St. Louis, MO
October 9, 2023

BIBLIOGRAPHY

Berger Burns Collection: The St. Louis Kaplan Feldman Holocaust Museum
https://stlholocaustmuseum.org

Gittel Burns: Oral histories and personal conversations: 2018-2023

Hochstadt, Steve. *Exodus to Shanghai*, Palgrave Macmillan, NY: 2012

Photo credits: Chagall, Marc. *Solitude,* 1933

NY Times: Secret History of Jews in Shanghai, 2019

On the cover: Walter Berger with his favorite dogs, Fifi and Mollie, in Beuthen, Germany, ca. 1935

ACKNOWLEDGMENTS

Diane Everman, for mentoring every step of this remarkable journey.

Paula Hanssen, for supportive guidance throughout, insbesondere die Handschriftenanalyse.

Gittel Burns and Cindy Burns Schrage, for unfettered access to the sources.

Martha K. Baker, Judy Vernick, and Ju Hyeon Han, for meticulous critiques of early drafts.

www.ingramcontent.com/pod-product-compliance
Lightning Source LLC
Chambersburg PA
CBHW050859240426
43673CB00026B/478/J